Help! I Can't Swim!

A Story About Safety In Water

Written by
Cindy Leaney

Illustrated by
Peter Wilks

Rourke

Publishing LLC
Vero Beach, Florida 32964

Before you read this story, take a look at the front cover of the book. Matt and José are trying to help someone in trouble.

1. What does José see that can rescue the boy in the water?

2. How are they practicing safety in water?

Produced by SGA Illustration and Design
Designed by Phil Kay
Series Editor: Frank Sloan

©2004 Rourke Publishing LLC

www.rourkepublishing.com

Library of Congress Cataloging-in-Publication Data

Leaney, Cindy.
    Help! I can't swim! : safety in water / by Cindy Leaney ; illustrated by Peter Wilks.
        p. cm. -- (Hero club safety)
    Summary: Matt and his friends head for the park and find themselves
helping to rescue a boy who cannot swim.
    ISBN 1-58952-743-7 (hardcover)
    1. Swimming--Safety measures--Juvenile literature. [1.
Swimming--Safety measures. 2. Safety.] I. Wilks, Peter, ill. II. Title.

GV838.53.S24L43 2003
797.2'1'0289--dc21

                                        2003003588

Printed in the USA

MP/W

Hi! I'm Makayla!

Hi! I'm Emily!

Hi! I'm Matt!

Hi! I'm José!

Welcome to The Hero Club!
Read about all the things that happen to them.
Try and guess what they'll do next.

www.theheroclub.com

"Cool kite, Matt."

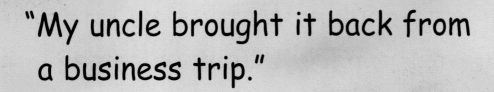

"My uncle brought it back from a business trip."

"Let's take it over to the park. We can go by Makayla's."

"Hi. We're taking Matt's new kite over to the park. Want to come?"

"Sure. I'll tell my mom. We'll be right down."

"Yeah, what's he doing? That's really dangerous!"

"It looks like he's trying to get his ball."

"He's going to fall in the water!"

"Quick, let's go down there."

"Come on, Em. Let's go get Mom."

"Don't go in the water yourselves, guys."

"I hope Matt doesn't try to jump in and save him."

"Me too. He's a good swimmer but Jonathan is scared. He could do something crazy."

"He fell in! There's a life preserver here someplace. There it is!"

"Don't worry, Jonathan!"

"I can't swim!"

"You'll be okay! The ring floats.
Hold on and kick to us. We'll help!"

"Don't be afraid. You'll be okay.
Just kick."

"Kayla's mom is coming, Matt.
I can see her."

"I wanted to get my ball."

"You could have drowned, you know."

"We were lucky you got here so fast, Mrs. Johnson."

WHAT DO YOU THINK?

Was it a good idea for Matt and José to stay out of the water?

Why or why not?

IMPORTANT IDEAS

On page 21, Matt and José say, "You'll be okay! The ring floats. Hold on and kick to us. We'll help!"

What would you do if you saw someone in trouble in the water?

Now that you have read this book, see if you can answer these questions:

1. What were the Hero Club kids taking to the park?

2. What was Jonathan trying to retrieve from the water and how was he trying to do this?

3. What do Makayla and Emily decide to do to help?

4. What do Matt and José give to Jonathan to help him?

About the author

Cindy Leaney teaches English and writes books for both young readers and adults. She has lived and worked in England, Kenya, Mexico, Saudi Arabia, and the United States.

About the illustrator

Peter Wilks began work in advertising, where he developed a love for illustration. He has drawn pictures for many children's books in Great Britain and in the United States.

HERO CLUB SAFETY SERIES

Do You Smell Smoke? (A Book About Safety with Fire)

Help! I Can't Swim! (A Book About Safety in Water)

Home Sweet Home (A Book About Safety at Home)

Long Walk to School (A Book About Bullying)

Look Out! (A Book About Safety on Bicycles)

Wrong Stop (A Book About Safety from Crime)